Not for Kids!

Hi there! I'm Milly.

I teach kids how to stay safe online
and seek help when they see
upsetting adult images.

Written by Liz Walker
Illustrated by Anita Mary

MW01134711

Parents, caregivers and professionals can access

Support Notes and Discussion Questions via

our website at www.notforkids.info

Dedicated to children around the world.

Not for Kids! helps children take charge of troubling

images and seek help from trusted adults.

Milly's my name and I'm not very old.

And when I feel curious, happy and bold

I love finding pictures, things old and things new.

Movies and images and photographs too.

Pictures are found everywhere that we go,

In museums and galleries, row after row.

Pictures on signs that can go on forever

Colours and shapes, all mixed in together.

My Mum puts pictures on her Facebook wall.

Our photos she shares with her friends but that's all.

Personal things should be kept face-to-face

To help keep the Internet helpful and safe.

Movies show pictures that move on the screen.

Sometimes I giggle and sometimes I scream.

They make me feel happy or make me feel sad

But I once saw a movie that made me feel bad.

At school on a phone - a movie was terrible!

It wasn't for me and it made me feel horrible.

Grown-ups doing things that I'd never seen.

Wiggly and icky – my tummy felt green.

I passed back the phone and said "I **don't** want to see!"

That video was bad and it wasn't for me!

I didn't feel certain of whom I should tell.

Confused and upset I was saved by the bell.

I went back to class and I tried to forget

Round and around; it played in my head.

Try as I might, I couldn't un-see.

That horrible movie kept troubling me.

Time to go home to my mum for warm hugs

To snuggle up close like a bug in a rug.

My tummy felt yuck and I wanted to cry.

I took a deep breath and let out a sigh.

Mum is so smart and is someone I trust.

I told her it all – as I knew that I must.

She cuddled me tightly and listened so well.

I let it all out – it felt so good to tell.

Mum calmed me down and she tried to explain

This wasn't my fault and I wasn't to blame.

A movie like that was not meant for my eyes

Or for anyone little or similar sized.

The things in that movie were really a bother.

It wasn't for me - what they did to each other.

I've learnt a good lesson and I know it is wise

To look away quickly or cover my eyes.

If movies or pictures have made me feel bad

I tell someone safe like my mum or my dad.

When horrible images are troubling my mind

I can move them along and leave them behind.

If I see some pictures that are not meant for me

I focus on breathing till I'm calm as can be.

Listening carefully for the quiet voice inside

That helps me make choices - it's my very own guide.

There'll always be pictures that swirl through my head

But I can take charge and tame them instead.

My brain is so clever it helps me to choose

The images to keep and the ones I should lose.

I still enjoy pictures and seeing what's nice

But for kids like me, I have important advice.

If you look at an image that's totally gross

Tell the safe adult that **you** trust the most.

For your mind to work calmly it needs to feel safe

And this keeps your heart in a happier place.

So catch yucky thoughts and give them the shove.

When you feel safe you will always feel loved.

"I love a rhyming children's book, and when great illustrations and an easy-to-read story combine to teach children about the yucky pictures they might see online and what to do if and when this happens - I'd say we're looking at a valuable resource for families and schools. A great educational tool for children and their trusted grown-ups."
Margie Buttriss, Founder of HUSHeducation

"It teaches you a lesson that you stand up for yourself and don't keep yucky bad things a secret. Just tell someone you trust and you won't get in trouble. I like that I now know what to do if a friend saw something and told me."
Abigail, 7 years old

"I love this story, it brought tears to my eyes. I had only just had a very deep and intense conversation with my 8yo about inappropriate stories she had been hearing from her older cousins, so this was incredibly timely for us. I think because she could identify so strongly with the little girl in this story, it helped her understand in a very safe way, that she isn't strange or bad for having all of the feelings that she had. I believe that many children will benefit from this beautiful, insightful and gentle story."
Shekinah, mum of 8 year old

From the author

When I was six years old, I came across some images of naked people that I knew were not for me. The images swirled around in my mind and really troubled my heart for quite some time. These inappropriate pictures gave me a wrong idea about behaviours, relationships and even myself.

I often wonder if things would have been different for me, if as a six year old I had talked to a trusted adult and asked for help. At the time however, I thought that by telling someone else, it would be me who got into trouble and I wasn't even sure anyone would have understood. How very wrong I was. As it turns out, asking for help would have been the very best thing I could have done.

These days troubling images can be found just about everywhere. Unfortunately, children of all ages can now be potentially exposed to inappropriate pictures and media on the Internet - images that their eyes were never meant to see.

My hope is that mums, dads, teachers, carers and safe grown up's everywhere will become more aware of online dangers and the impact that unsafe images have on our children's lives.

Not for kids! was written to inspire and facilitate educated and healthy conversation regarding sexual imagery.

The goal - to empower children to take charge of troubling images, reach out and speak to a trusted adult, and to enable young people to listen to their inner voice that helps keep their heart in a happier place.

Liz Walker is a mother of three, sexuality educator, young people's advocate, author and professional speaker. To learn more about Liz, visit www.lizwalkerpresents.com. To access educational resources and support for schools visit www.youthwellbeingproject.com.au.

Not for Kids!
Published by Walker Inspirations
PO Box 1055, North Lakes
Queensland, 4509 Australia
www.notforkids.info

First published in 2016

ISBN number 9780958027939

Text copyright © Liz Walker, 2016
Illustration copyright © Anita Mary, 2016

Written by Liz Walker
Illustrated by Anita Mary
Typesetting and Layout by Toni Esser

All rights reserved. No part of this book may be reproduced, stored in a retrieval system, or transmitted in any form or by any means, electronic, mechanical, photocopying, recording or otherwise without the prior permission in writing from Walker Inspirations.

Made in United States
North Haven, CT
31 July 2023

39770987R00015